The South China Sea in Focus

Clarifying the Limits of Maritime Dispute

AUTHOR
Gregory B. Poling

A Report of the CSIS Sumitro Chair for Southeast Asia Studies

July 2013

50 YEARS | CHARTING OUR FUTURE

CSIS | CENTER FOR STRATEGIC & INTERNATIONAL STUDIES

ROWMAN & LITTLEFIELD
Lanham • Boulder • New York • Toronto • Plymouth, UK

About CSIS—50th Anniversary Year

For 50 years, the Center for Strategic and International Studies (CSIS) has developed solutions to the world's greatest policy challenges. As we celebrate this milestone, CSIS scholars are developing strategic insights and bipartisan policy solutions to help decisionmakers chart a course toward a better world.

CSIS is a nonprofit organization headquartered in Washington, D.C. The Center's 220 full-time staff and large network of affiliated scholars conduct research and analysis and develop policy initiatives that look into the future and anticipate change.

Founded at the height of the Cold War by David M. Abshire and Admiral Arleigh Burke, CSIS was dedicated to finding ways to sustain American prominence and prosperity as a force for good in the world. Since 1962, CSIS has become one of the world's preeminent international institutions focused on defense and security; regional stability; and transnational challenges ranging from energy and climate to global health and economic integration.

CSIS does not take specific policy positions; accordingly, all views expressed herein should be understood to be solely those of the author(s).

Library of Congress Cataloging-in-Publication Data
CIP information available on request.

ISBN: 978-1-4422-2485-8 (pb); 978-1-4422-2486-5 (eBook)

Center for Strategic & International Studies
1800 K Street, NW, Washington, DC 20006
202-887-0200 | www.csis.org

Rowman & Littlefield
4501 Forbes Boulevard, Lanham, MD 20706
301-459-3366 | www.rowman.com

Contents

Acknowledgments

Only in recent years has sufficient information entered the public domain to make an analysis like this by a nonprofit think tank possible. There is a community of people around the globe performing legal and geospatial analyses of the South China Sea disputes—more than I can name here—and their contributions to the field were invaluable while completing this project.

I would like to thank CSIS Sumitro Chair for Southeast Asia Studies Ernest Bower and the Chair's deputy director, Murray Hiebert, for seeing the value in this project and facilitating it. I would also like to thank my colleagues Mary Beth Jordan, Elke Larsen, and Kathleen Rustici. This report was made possible by the initial research of Kiet Nguyen at CSIS, as well as by the talents of Michael Mahoney and Sohayla Pruitt at Digital Globe. I am also grateful to Alison Bours and James Dunton for this report's production.

Finally, I would like to extend a special thanks to the Japan Aerospace Exploration Agency for generously supporting this project.

Abbreviations and Acronyms

CLCS	Commission on the Limits of the Continental Shelf
CNOOC	China National Offshore Oil Corporation
EEZ	exclusive economic zone
ICJ	International Court of Justice
ITLOS	International Tribunal for the Law of the Sea
UNCLOS	United Nations Convention on the Law of the Sea

Executive Summary

The complexity of maritime and territorial disputes in the South China Sea is nothing short of mind-numbing. They involve six countries—Brunei, China, Malaysia, the Philippines, Taiwan, and Vietnam—hundreds of tiny land features, and a body of international law that is both contested and complicated to interpret. The result has been decades of impasse. But it is an impasse that this report seeks to take a small step toward breaking.

The overlapping claims to the islands and smaller land features in the sea are unresolvable in the short to medium term. There is nothing in the UN Convention on the Law of the Sea (UNCLOS) to resolve sovereignty disputes over land and no chance that the claimants will submit their claims to the International Court of Justice or another arbitration body. The good faith and willingness to make concessions that would be needed to negotiate the claims to the features do not exist.

But the fact that the land disputes in the South China Sea are unalterable does not mean that the disputes over its waters are as well. UNCLOS has nothing to say on the territorial disputes, but it has plenty to say about the maritime disagreements. Maritime claims under international law are determined by sovereignty over land, so as long as there are disputes over the land features of the South China Sea, there will be disputes over the waters. But that does not mean that the area of dispute cannot be clarified. And that clarification is critical to managing tensions in the region.

This report blends analysis of maritime law, satellite imagery, public source data, and geographic information systems to clarify the areas under dispute. The result is the following map, which shows the maximum area of the South China Sea that is legally in dispute. This map and all others printed in this report are approximations of shapefiles created by the author. For those looking for greater accuracy or to perform analyses of their own, all of the shapefiles are available for download at http://csis.org/program/south-china-sea-high-resolution.

This map differs significantly from those charts most often used to depict the South China Sea dispute, and the methodology used to create it is explained at length in this report. But the most important differences are that it is smaller than China's infamous "nine-dash line" map depicting its claim and that it is founded entirely on international

Figure 1. Maximum area of legal dispute

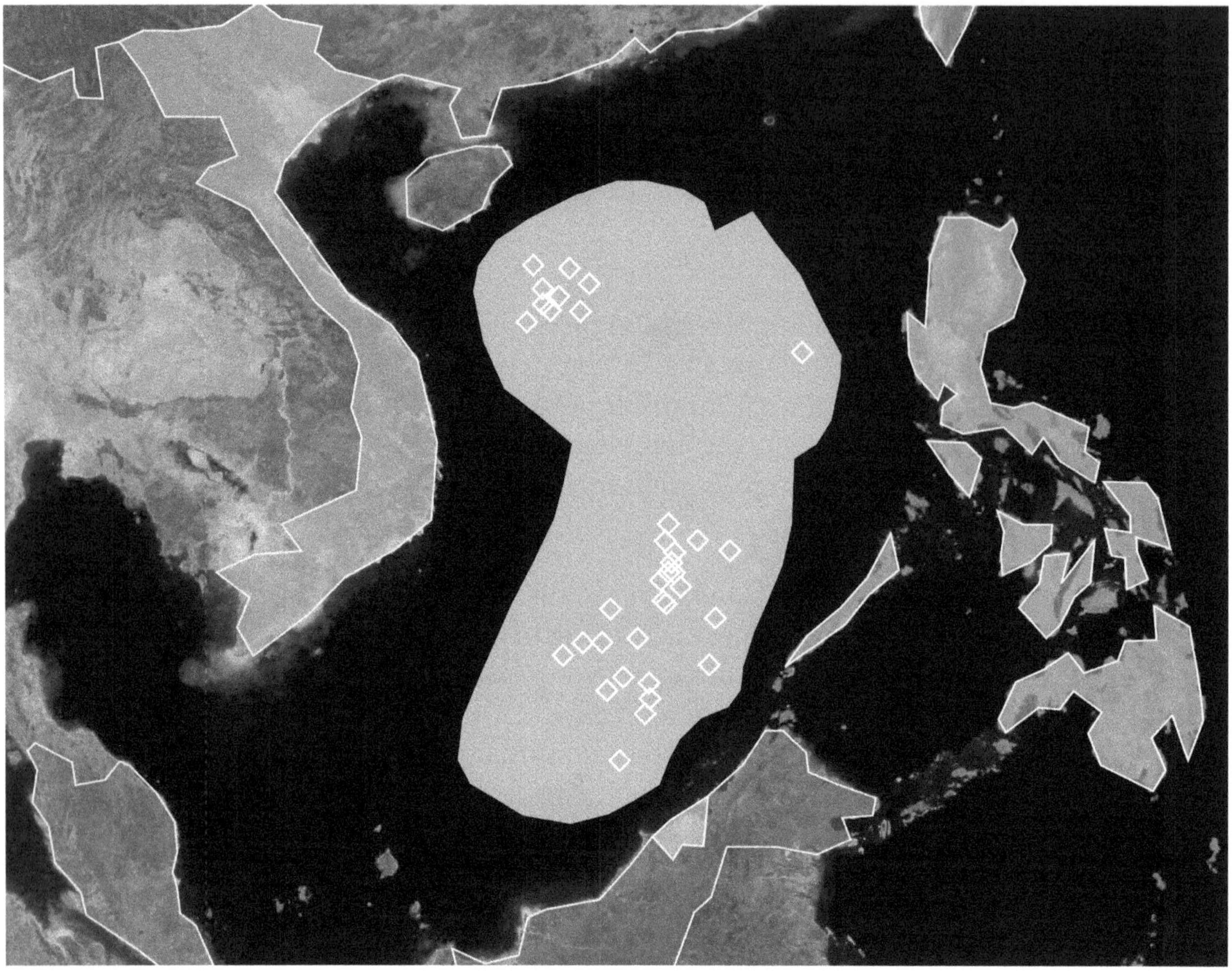

law. Those differences are key to finding a workable means of managing the South China Sea disputes.

The best and likely only real hope of tamping down tensions in the absence of an actual settlement of claims in the South China Sea is joint development of the disputed resources. This must include both fisheries and oil and gas resources. Rivalry over these resources has been the immediate cause of most of the policing incidents, military clashes, and arrests of fishermen in the sea in recent years. Any successful effort to jointly develop resources must include China, the heavy hitter in the area and the provocateur of most episodes of violence in recent years.

Of course, it is impossible to develop disputed resources jointly if the claimants cannot agree on what is disputed. And in this area Beijing is the odd man out. Thanks to the purposeful ambiguity of China's claims, Beijing essentially classifies any resources it wants as

Figure 2. China National Offshore Oil Corporation blocks

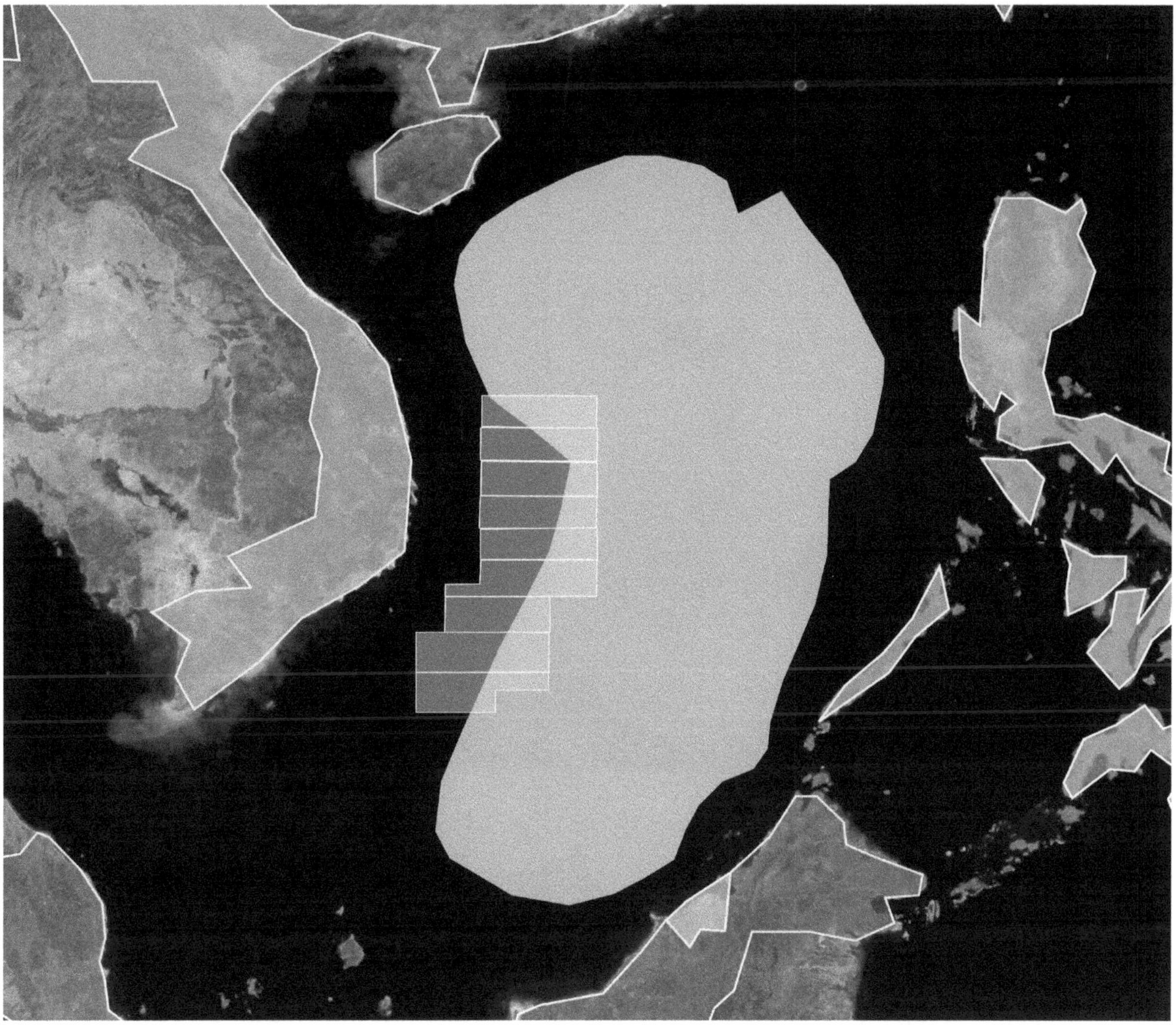

lying within disputed waters. Fellow claimants are, naturally, unwilling to offer joint development of resources just miles off their shores when China will not do the same. This is especially true when the area allegedly under dispute unambiguously falls under the sovereignty of one or another claimant under international law.

China's insistence that essentially all the waters in the South China Sea fall within its jurisdiction, without providing any legal rationale, has led to several disputes over oil and gas concessions. For instance, on June 25, 2012, the state-owned China National Offshore Oil Corporation (CNOOC) responded to ongoing tensions with Vietnam by declaring nine new offshore oil and gas blocks open for bids from foreign companies. The blocks were off the coast of Vietnam, and the closest was located 230 nautical miles from China. All nine

Figure 3. Philippine and Vietnamese blocks

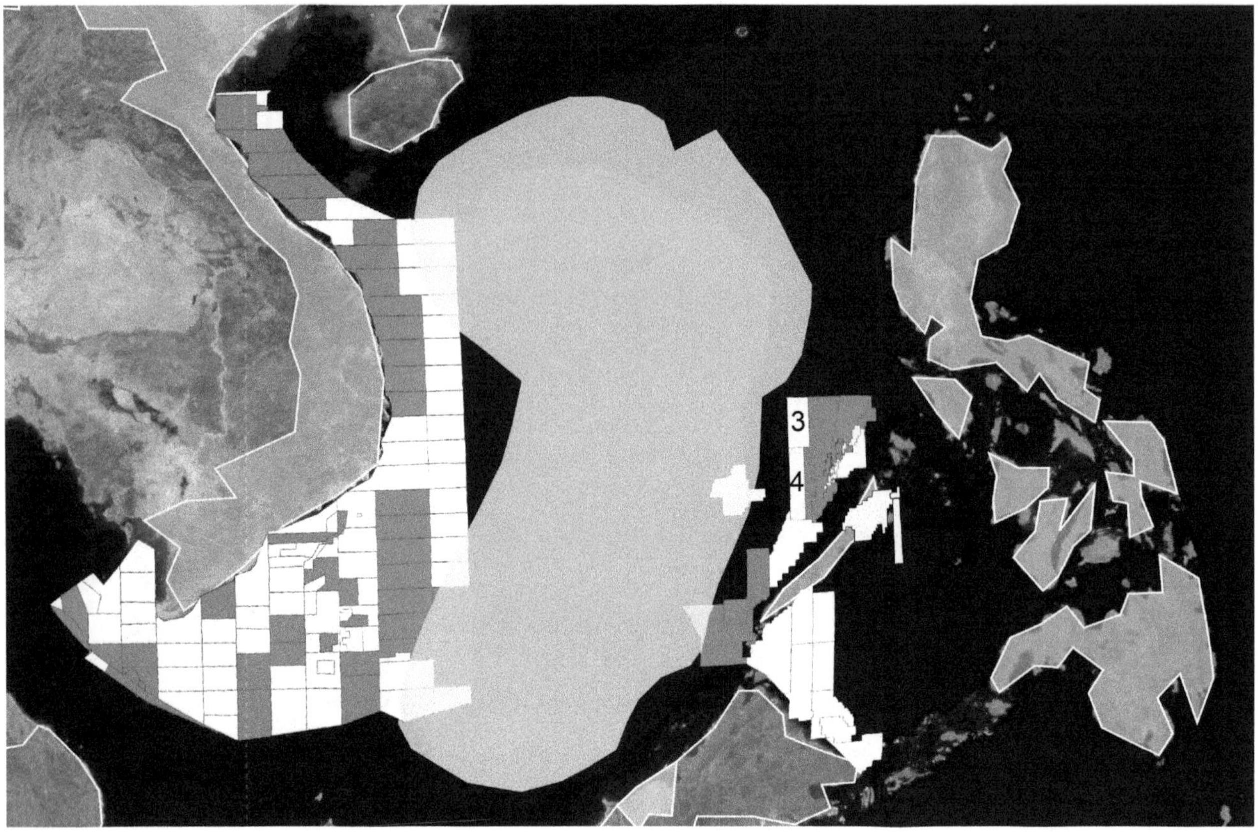

also overlapped with blocks previously created by Vietnam and leased to foreign companies, including ExxonMobil.

By simply overlaying these blocks with the map of the maximum legal dispute, it is obvious that CNOOC has no basis to claim most of the area that it put out for bid.

A few months earlier, on February 29, 2012, the Philippines had invited foreign companies to take part in its long awaited fourth energy contracting round. This round opened bidding on 15 oil and gas blocks, two of which—Areas 3 and 4—drew protests from Beijing. Even though the blocks were just off the Philippine coast and hundreds of miles from China, Beijing claimed they were within its legal maritime jurisdiction.

However, Figure 3 shows that the vast majority of oil and gas blocks created by Vietnam and the Philippines, including Areas 3 and 4, lie entirely in undisputed waters.

Rights to oil and gas is only one aspect of the South China Sea dispute that is clarified by determining the maximum area of legal dispute, but it is one of particular importance. It is also accurately treated as the keystone of potential joint development in the area. If joint development is not restricted to the disputed area, along the lines shown in Figure 3, it will never get off the ground.

Chapter 1 of this report provides an introduction to the South China Sea disputes and argues for the necessity of clarifying claims.

Chapter 2 maps the legal claims of each of the claimant countries, without taking into consideration the unresolvable land features in the sea.

Chapter 3 introduces the impact of the unresolvable land features on the claims and determines the maximum area of legal dispute.

1 Background

The South China Sea is the site of one of the globe's most contentious, and probably its most complicated, sovereignty disputes. Six countries—Brunei, China, Malaysia, the

Figure 4. The South China Sea claimants[1]

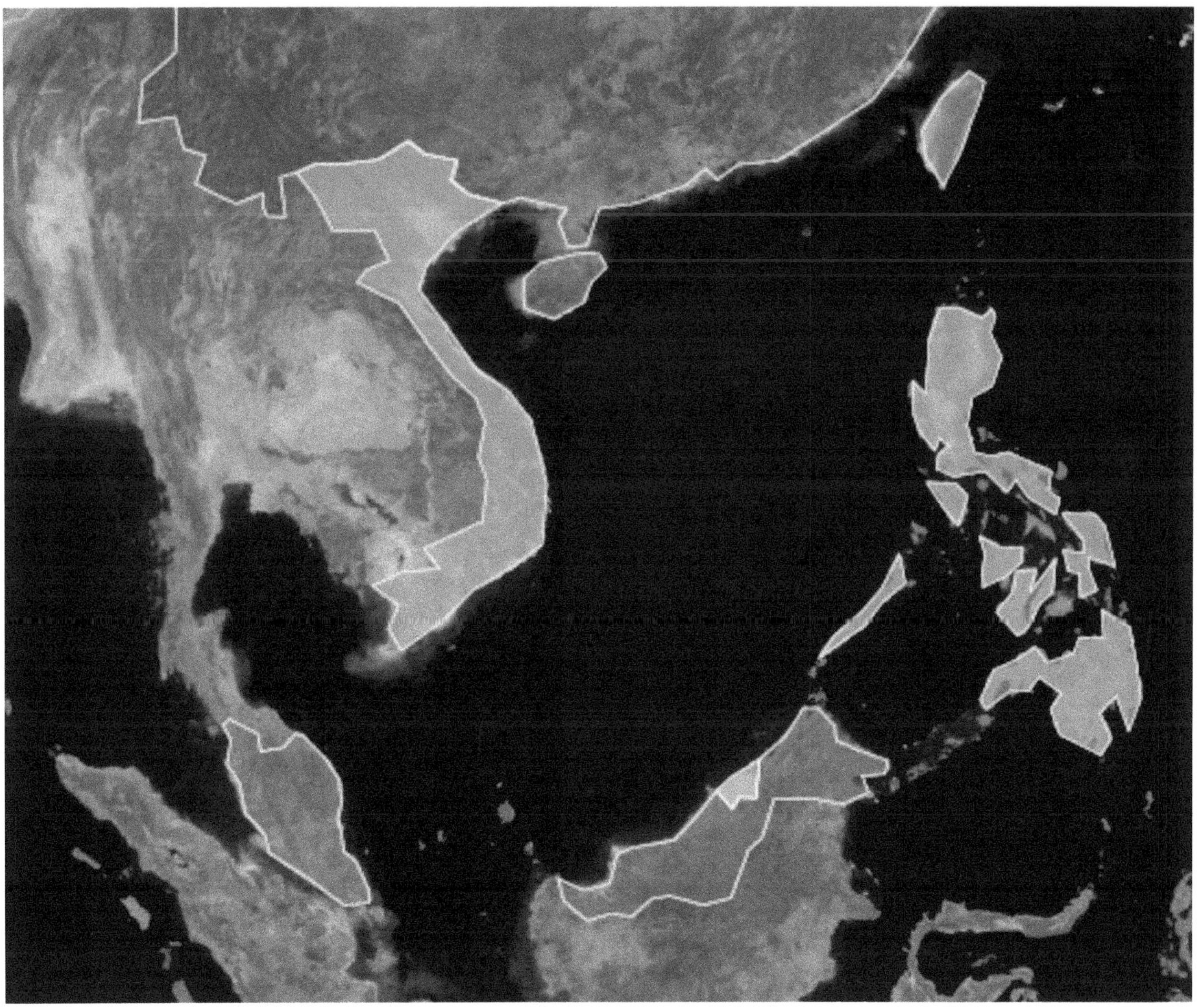

1. This map and all others printed in this report are approximations of shapefiles created by the author. For those looking for greater accuracy or to perform analyses of their own, all of the shapefiles are available for download at http://csis.org/program/south-china-sea-high-resolution.

Philippines, Taiwan, and Vietnam—maintain overlapping claims to the waters and tiny land features of the sea. The dispute has flared hot and cold for decades, most often between China on the one hand and one or more of the other claimants on the other. This is because China's claims are by far the most extensive.

The current round of tensions in the South China Sea can be traced to the 2009 joint submission to the United Nations by Vietnam and Malaysia of a section of their extended continental shelves in the area.[2] China responded by submitting an objection to the UN Commission on the Limits of the Continental Shelf (CLCS) decrying Vietnamese and Malaysian infringement of its claims, which it defined via an ambiguous map that encompassed nearly the entire sea.[3] This claim was depicted in the now-infamous nine-dash line map.

Ambiguity: The Enemy of Progress

Ambiguity over the claims in the South China Sea does not serve anyone's interests. All the claimants are guilty of failing to fully clarify their claims according to international law, but the most ambiguous by far are Beijing's positions. It is important to note the use of the plural "positions," because there is scant agreement as to what precisely the Chinese position is. In fact, Chinese policy amounts to avoiding taking a position at all costs. Without a defined Chinese position, identifying areas for potential cooperation and eventually resolving claims is not possible.

China's policy of strategic ambiguity, as it has been euphemistically called, serves its purposes well. It allows China the flexibility to interpret its position to serve the audience at hand. This is why the Ministry of Foreign Affairs was able to issue its well-publicized statement in February 2012 stating that no nation claims sovereignty over the entire South China Sea and that the dispute is only about the "islands and adjacent waters."[4] This raised hopes in the United States and among the other Asian claimants that China was backing away from claiming all the waters within the nine-dash line and moving to bring its position in line with international law.

That, however, has clearly not been the case. Continued Chinese objections to the activities of other claimants that occur far outside the possible "adjacent waters" of any islands or other features in the South China Sea prove that the government is not restricting itself to the Ministry of Foreign Affairs' position.

---

2. Malaysia and the Socialist Republic of Vietnam, Joint Submission to the Commission on the Limits of the Continental Shelf Pursuant to Article 76, Paragraph 8 of the United Nations Convention on the Law of the Sea 1982 in Respect of the Southern Part of the South China Sea (May 2009), http://www.un.org/Depts/los/clcs_new/submissions_files/submission_mysvnm_33_2009.htm.

3. People's Republic of China, Note Verbale CML/17/2009 (May 7, 2009), http://www.un.org/Depts/los/clcs_new/submissions_files/mysvnm33_09/chn_2009re_mys_vnm_e.pdf.

4. Ministry of Foreign Affairs of the People's Republic of China, "Foreign Ministry Spokesperson Hong Lei's Regular Press Conference on February 29, 2012," March 1, 2012, http://www.fmprc.gov.cn/eng/xwfw/s2510/t910855.htm.

These developments highlight the need for the Association of Southeast Asian Nations (ASEAN) claimants—Vietnam, the Philippines, Malaysia, and Brunei—to take a stand on what is genuinely in dispute in the South China Sea and what is not. As long as that fundamental fact remains unclear, China will continue to employ ambiguous and contradictory claims to pursue its interests in the South China Sea at the expense of its smaller neighbors.

Some steps have been taken in this direction. Vietnam and Malaysia's 2009 joint submission of their southern extended continental shelves to the CLCS was an important first step in this effort. The Philippines baseline law, passed the same year, establishing its coastal baselines in accordance with the UN Convention on the Law of the Sea (UNCLOS), was another.[5]

Despite these steps, too much remains ambiguous in the South China Sea. Vietnam's National Assembly in 2012 passed a Law of the Sea reiterating its claim to the Paracels and Spratlys, but it remains unclear just what Vietnam is claiming in the maritime domain.[6] Beyond its southern boundary with Malaysia, what extended continental shelf is it claiming? Does it consider the islands of the Spratlys and Paracels capable of generating a 200-nautical-mile exclusive economic zone (EEZ) or not? The same questions must be asked and answered by the other three Southeast Asian claimants—Brunei, Malaysia, and the Philippines.

The Path Forward

The best and likely only real hope of tamping down tensions in the absence of an actual settlement of claims in the South China Sea is joint development of the disputed resources. This must include both fisheries and oil and gas resources. Of course, it is impossible to jointly develop disputed resources if the claimants cannot agree on what is disputed. Thanks to the purposeful ambiguity of China's claims, Beijing essentially claims that any resource it wants lies in disputed waters. Fellow claimants are, naturally, unwilling to offer joint development of resources just miles off their shores when China will not do the same. This is especially true when the area allegedly under dispute unambiguously falls under the sovereignty of one or another claimant under international law.

The Southeast Asian parties have seen their positions on many of these questions slowly converge. For instance, all four appear to operate under the assumption that the Spratlys and Paracels are not legally islands but merely rocks and therefore entitled only to a 12-nautical-mile territorial sea.

An honest effort to resolve or even manage the disputes in the South China Sea requires that this and other assumptions be codified in law. This does not mean that any of the

5. Republic of the Philippines, Republic Act No. 9522 (March 10, 2009), http://www.lawphil.net/statutes/repacts/ra2009/ra_9522_2009.html.

6. Vietnam, The Law of the Sea of Viet Nam (June 21, 2012), trans. BienDong.net, http://biendong.net/en/documents/law/309-the-law-of-the-sea-of-viet-nam.html.

claimants have to give up anything regarding their claims to the features in the South China Sea. Instead, it would allow them to strengthen the legal basis of their maritime claims and separate the far more intractable but geographically much smaller territorial disputes. Most important, it would allow them to present a united front to China in arguing one crucial point: The only acceptable basis for maritime claims in the South China Sea must be international law, especially UNCLOS.

Were the Southeast Asian claimants to present an agreed-upon framework for establishing what is and is not disputed, the burden would rest with Beijing to clarify the basis for its own claims. At that point, Beijing would have limited options. Such pressure might give more moderate voices, like those in the Ministry of Foreign Affairs, more credibility, allowing China to clarify its claims by retaining those to the Spratlys and Paracels but giving up its egregious claims to the waters in between. This would mark an important step toward resolving the South China Sea disputes.

Alternatively, Beijing could reject entirely the primacy of accepted international law in the dispute, but that would be extremely damaging to China's larger interests. Beijing would more likely refuse to engage in any dialogue at all. Although possible in the short term, such a course of action would identify China as the undeniable remaining belligerent in the dispute and rally regional and international opinion around the Southeast Asian claimants' position. Eventually, China would likely find it less damaging to its reputation and interests to clarify its claims than to cling to its traditional ambiguity.

It is time for the Southeast Asian claimants to fully codify, both in domestic legislation and in a multilateral framework, what is and is not in dispute under international law. That would be a position that the international community, including the United States, could legitimately support because it would mean not defending the claims of any individual party to the dispute but rather supporting international law itself.

2 Identifying the Claims

As long as ambiguity of claims is the rule rather than the exception in the South China Sea, the simplest steps toward a solution will prove impossible. Joint development of oil and gas resources is off the table for most because China offers to pursue such activities only in areas that the Southeast Asian claimants do not consider legally in dispute. Beijing, meanwhile, refuses to discuss joint development in those areas that all claimants are agreed are disputed, specifically those areas of the seabed in the immediate vicinity of the Spratlys and Paracels.

The same principle applies to fisheries. Run-ins between fishermen and authorities from around the region are a perennial issue, at least in part because the claimants do not hold the same definition of which waters are and are not disputed.

The sole basis for clarifying these claims must be UNCLOS, to which China and the Southeast Asian claimants all are signatories.[1] The convention is crystal clear that its provisions are paramount for all areas that they cover.[2] Therefore, unless UNCLOS has nothing to say on a specific issue, all the South China Sea claimants are legally bound to base their maritime claims on it.

With this axiom as a starting point, this report uses relatively simple geospatial analysis to delimit which areas are and are not legally in dispute. The maps in the following chapters will narrow the area in dispute until the maximum area of dispute is found. But a final resolution of that question lies with the claimants themselves or with an international arbitration mechanism of their choice, not with this author.

The Textbook Version

The vast majority of maps publicly available for the South China Sea claims are outdated and involve a great deal of guesswork. This is an unfortunate effect of the ambiguity of claims by all the parties involved. One more-or-less standard depiction of the claims, what this report calls the "textbook version," is shown in Figure 5.

1. This report treats Taiwan's claim to the nine-dash line as identical to China's because neither has made any moves to distinguish their respective claims or bring them into line with international law.

2. UN Convention on the Law of the Sea (UNCLOS), December 10, 1982, Articles 309–311, https://www.un.org/depts/los/convention_agreements/texts/unclos/UNCLOS-TOC.htm.

Figure 5. The textbook map

The textbook version features China's nine-dash line claim as included in its note to the CLCS in 2009. It also features a Malaysian claim that is partly founded upon boundaries agreed on with Indonesia in 1969,[3] with Thailand in 1979,[4] and demarcated by the 1898

3. U.S. Department of State, "Indonesia-Malaysia Continental Shelf Boundary," International Boundary Study, Series A, Limits in the Seas, No. 1 (January 21, 1970), http://www.law.fsu.edu/library/collection/LimitsinSeas/ls001.pdf.

4. Treaty between the Kingdom of Thailand and Malaysia Relating to the Delimitation of the Territorial Seas of the Two Countries, October 24, 1979, http://www.un.org/Depts/los/LEGISLATIONANDTREATIES

Treaty of Paris that ceded the Philippines to the United States from Spain.[5] The remainder is based on a 1979 map of Malaysia's continental shelf published by the government in Kuala Lumpur,[6] but never properly explained or submitted to the CLCS. Malaysia also claims an EEZ from its coastline,[7] but has never clarified the boundary of this zone, which would overlap with that of its neighbors at every point. The Malaysian claim on the textbook map also cuts across Brunei's maritime claim, implying that Kuala Lumpur does not recognize it.

In the case of the Philippines, the claim most often shown predates the 2009 law the country passed to clarify its baselines. Instead, it shows a claim based mostly on the Treaty of Paris, with the addition of a large bulge around most of the Spratlys, or the Kalayaan Islands Group as it is known in the Philippines.[8] This so-called Kalayaan box was done away with by the same 2009 law, but that fact is often overlooked.

Vietnam's claim on the textbook map is also outdated. Hanoi has defined its territorial baselines,[9] though they are not widely accepted by the international community, but it has never clarified its EEZ or the entirety of its continental shelf. In lieu of such data, the textbook map starts with a map of proposed petroleum concession blocks that Hanoi drew up in the 1970s.[10] Those blocks have long since been abandoned in favor of concessions that fall entirely within the 200 nautical miles Vietnam can claim for an EEZ from its coast. But the fact that Vietnam claims the entirety of both the Paracel and Spratly Islands, and that the 1970s map encompasses both, has led most to leave the extensive line in place.

Brunei's claim according to the textbook map is the only one with a claim to legality. It is based on three things: (1) its maritime boundaries with Malaysia as defined in two

---

/PDFFILES/TREATIES/THA-MYS1979TS.PDF; Memorandum of Understanding between the Kingdom of Thailand and Malaysia on the Delimitation of the Continental Shelf Boundary between the Two Countries in the Gulf of Thailand, October 24, 1979, http://www.un.org/Depts/los/LEGISLATIONANDTREATIES/PDFFILES/TREATIES /THA-MYS1979CS.PDF.

5. Lowell B. Bautista, "The Philippine Treaty Limits and Territorial Waters Claim in International Law," *Social Science Diliman* (January 2008–December 2009): 110, http://journals.upd.edu.ph/index.php/social sciencediliman/article/viewFile/2046/1956. The Philippines–Malaysia maritime boundary demarcated by the Treaty of Paris was made without the consultation of Britain during the colonial period or Malaysia following independence. But neither objected to the boundary, and Malaysia subsequently recognized it via its 1979 map. A separate 1930 treaty demarcated the Philippines–Malaysia boundary in the Sulu Sea, but that falls outside the geographical scope of this report.

6. *Peta menunjukkan sempadan perairan dan pelantar benua Malaysia* [Map showing the territorial waters and continental shelf of Malaysia] (Kuala Lumpur: Directorate of National Mapping Malaysia, 1979).

7. Malaysia, like Brunei, has never legally declared straight territorial baselines from which its EEZ would be measured. The map it submitted with its 2009 joint continental shelf submission showed straight baselines, but where they lie is unclear. China, the Philippines, and Vietnam have declared baselines.

8. Republic of the Philippines, Presidential Decree No. 1596—Declaring Certain Area Part of the Philippine Territory and Providing for Their Government and Administration (June 11, 1978), http://www.verafiles.org /docs/pd1596.pdf.

9. Socialist Republic of Viet Nam, Statement of 12 November 1982 by the Government of the Socialist Republic of Viet Nam on the Territorial Sea Baseline of Viet Nam (November 12, 1982), http://www.un.org/Depts /los/LEGISLATIONANDTREATIES/PDFFILES/VNM_1982_Statement.pdf.

10. Mark J. Valencia, Jon M. Van Dyke, and Noel A. Ludwig, *Sharing the Resources of the South China Sea* (Honolulu: University of Hawaii Press, 1999), 11–12.

British Orders in Council in 1958;[11] (2) the extension of that boundary as an EEZ out to 200 nautical miles, as declared in 1982 and accepted by Malaysia in 2009;[12] and (3) the extension of those boundaries for an extended continental shelf, approximately 60 nautical miles farther according to an official 1988 map.[13] Brunei has not presented evidence for its claim to an extended continental shelf, but it did declare its intention to do so in 2009.[14]

In order to clarify each of the littoral states' legal claims in the South China Sea and properly delimit the maximum area in dispute, it is necessary to tackle each claimant, except Brunei, one at a time. The remaining sections will begin that process by determining the legal claims of each state from their coastlines. The effect of the disputed islands, rocks, and other features on the parties' claims will be dealt with in Chapter 3.

Malaysia

Malaysia's actual claims to the South China Sea are relatively easy to clarify. As shown in the textbook map, Malaysia has delimited much of its maritime boundary with Indonesia's Tudjuh Archipelago and with the Philippines.[15] No progress has been made in delimiting the boundary between Vietnam's continental shelf and that of mainland Malaysia to the west of its boundaries with the Tudjuh Archipelago. The claim that Malaysia made on that section of continental shelf in 1979 therefore still stands. It should be noted, though, that this claim is roughly halfway between Vietnam's baselines and the Malaysian coast, so it is likely close to the spot of any final settlement.

The only real change in Malaysia's claim is the shift in the extended continental shelf it claims from the states of Sabah and Sarawak on the island of Borneo. As noted, Vietnam and Malaysia in 2009 made a joint submission to the CLCS, which covered this section of continental shelf. The two did not actually delimit the boundary between them. Both instead agreed to claim the other's 200-nautical-mile EEZ limit as the border of their own continental shelf. The area of resulting overlap has been set aside for joint development in lieu of demarcation.

The status of the boundaries between Malaysia's and Brunei's continental shelf claims remains ambiguous. Both countries have agreed that Brunei is entitled to a 200-nautical-mile EEZ, but Malaysia has never conceded that Brunei is also entitled to an

---

11. North Borneo (Definition of Boundaries) Order in Council, 1958, Statutory Instruments 1958 No. 1517; Sarawak (Definition of Boundaries) Order in Council, 1958, Statutory Instruments 1958 No. 1518, cited in Brunei Darussalam, Preliminary Submission Concerning the Outer Limits of Its Continental Shelf (2009), http://www.un.org/Depts/los/clcs_new/submissions_files/preliminary/brn2009preliminaryinformation.pdf.

12. Brunei Darussalam, Preliminary Submission, 3.

13. Valencia, Van Dyke, and Ludwig, *Sharing the Resources of the South China Sea*, 38.

14. Brunei Darussalam, Preliminary Submission, 7.

15. Further discussion of Malaysia's boundaries with Singapore and Thailand falls outside the geographical scope of this report.

Figure 6. Malaysia's legal claim

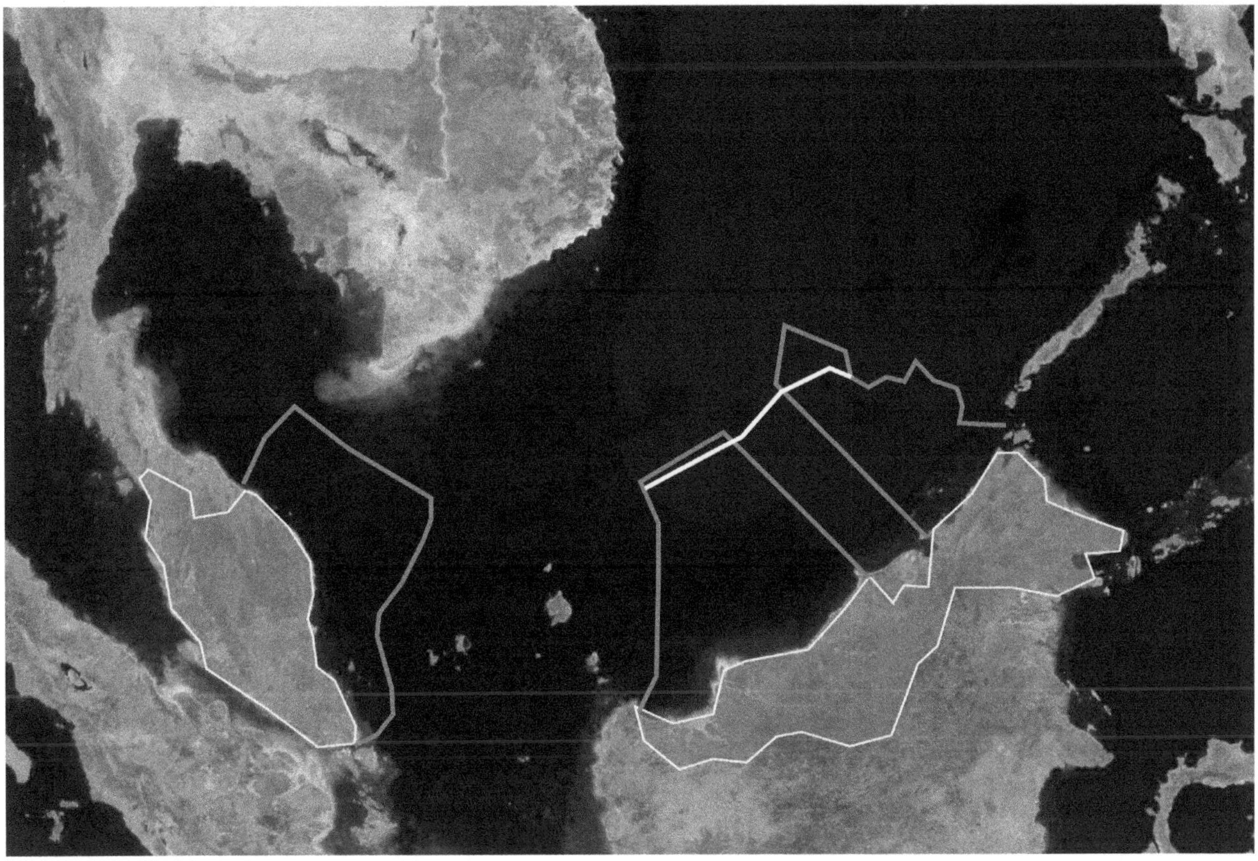

extension of is continental shelf beyond 200 nautical miles. As shown in Figure 6, Malaysia's joint submission of its continental shelf claim with Vietnam shows an unbroken line, implicitly denying Brunei's right to extend its shelf to the same distance, much less beyond it. Common sense says this is impossible under UNCLOS: the geography of the island of Borneo cannot generate an extended continental shelf for Malaysia but fail to do so for Brunei. Malaysia's continental shelf claim must therefore have a gap to accommodate Brunei's shelf.

The difference between Malaysia's actual legal claims in the South China Sea (red) and the claims most often depicted for it (white) are shown in Figure 6.

The Philippines

Whereas recent adjustments to Malaysia's maritime claims involved only a small change to its continental shelf, the task is much more difficult for the Philippines. This is partly because Manila's former South China Sea claims, as depicted in the textbook map, were woefully out of step with accepted international law, and UNCLOS in particular.

For years, the Philippines maintained the lines established by the Treaty of Paris and treated them as if they were a claim to territorial waters. As such a claim is possible only within 12 nautical miles of a country's shores, the position was in desperate need of change. The same was true of the randomly drawn box surrounding the Kalayaan Islands Group in the Spratlys.

Luckily, Manila recognized that the illegality of its own claims was undermining its position in the South China Sea by opening it to the same charges it was leveling against Beijing. To remedy this, it passed its landmark baselines law in 2009. The law took two critical steps toward clarifying Philippine claims:

1. It declared that Manila claims a 12-nautical-mile territorial sea and an EEZ of up to 200 nautical miles from straight territorial baselines between coordinates enumerated in the law. It is worth noting that the Philippines' baselines, though not above reproach, have not drawn the charges of illegality that Vietnam's and China's have.

2. The law did away with the "Kalayaan box," declaring that, although Manila still lays claim to the islands and other features within it, it does so only via UNCLOS's "Regime of Islands."[16] This means that the Philippines claims only the waters generated by the land features within the Kalayaan Group, not all the waters in the former box. Manila has not defined which features are above water at high tide and therefore generate a 12-nautical-mile territorial sea or which, if any, also generate an EEZ and continental shelf by meeting the UNCLOS definition of an "island." That definition will be discussed at greater length in Chapter 3.

As a result of the 2009 baselines law, the Philippines legal maritime claims in the South China Sea are now much clearer. A section of its southern boundary with Malaysia remains determined by the Treaty of Paris. But the vast majority of its South China Sea claims are now determined by the EEZs generated from its territorial baselines.

Most of the Philippines' legal maritime claim in the South China Sea extends a full 200 nautical miles. The two areas where this is not the case are in the south and north, where it runs into the claims of Malaysia and China/Taiwan,[17] respectively. Malaysia and the Philippines have not demarcated the majority of their EEZs and continental shelves in the South China Sea. The same is true of the Philippines on the one hand and Taiwan and China on the other. Because this is the case, Manila could in theory put forth a claim to an EEZ of 200 nautical miles or to the limit of an adjacent or opposite country's territorial sea, whichever is closer. But it would do so recognizing full well that the claim is not really "legal."

---

16. UNCLOS, Article 121.

17. As it does with the nine-dash line, this report treats the legal maritime claims of China and Taiwan as identical. This is because both officially claim the entirety of mainland China and the island of Taiwan as their territory. Should the government of Taiwan forsake its claim to mainland China, or vice versa, this approach would warrant revisiting.

Under UNCLOS, every coastal state has the right to an EEZ and continental shelf, a right of which no other country can deprive it. The convention calls on states with overlapping claims to delimit these boundaries in such a way as to "achieve an equitable solution."[18] This means that in the case of two opposing coastlines, one country laying claim to 80 percent of the intervening water is illegal because it is clearly not equitable. The principle of equity has been enshrined repeatedly by international tribunals as the legally necessary determinate in delimiting EEZs and continental shelves, most recently in the International Tribunal for the Law of the Sea's 2012 ruling on the boundary between Myanmar and Bangladesh in the Bay of Bengal.[19]

Admittedly, equity can be a slippery concept. A claim to 80 percent of the waters between two states is not equitable, but does that mean that a 50–50 split necessarily is? If one opposing coast is considerably longer than another, it could warrant a larger maritime claim. This was the principle on which Vietnam and China agreed in 2004 to delimit their maritime boundaries in the Gulf of Tonkin, with Vietnam receiving 53.23 percent of the area and China 46.77 percent.[20] The same is true if one coast is so deeply concave that an equidistant line of delimitation would severely disadvantage it. The severe concavity of the Bangladeshi coastline is the reason that the International Tribunal for the Law of the Sea (ITLOS) chose to adjust the equidistant line between it and Myanmar.[21]

Nevertheless, ITLOS, the International Court of Justice (ICJ), and Arbitral Tribunals set up under UNCLOS have all ruled repeatedly that equidistance must be taken as the starting point for delimitation of maritime boundaries and adjusted only if the resulting line is then found to be inequitable.[22] Therefore, where the Philippines' maritime claims in the South China Sea overlap with those of Malaysia and Taiwan, a 50–50 split must be assumed equitable unless proven otherwise.

Concavity is not an issue in the case of the Philippines' coastline opposite Malaysia or Taiwan. The effect of the length of opposing coastlines on equity is impossible to gauge unless decided by an international court or through bilateral negotiation. None of the countries in question have ever argued that their coastlines make an equidistant line unfair. Any outside attempt to do so is further complicated by the Philippines' declared archipelagic baselines, which may or may not be deemed legal by an international body or by its neighbors. The Philippines' legal claim in the areas in question is therefore

18. UNCLOS, Articles 74 and 83.

19. International Tribunal for the Law of the Sea (ITLOS), Case 16—Dispute Concerning Delimitation of the Maritime Boundary between Bangladesh and Myanmar in the Bay of Bengal, Judgment (March 14, 2012), 61, 72, http://www.itlos.org/fileadmin/itlos/documents/cases/case_no_16/C16_Judgment_14_03_2012_rev.pdf.

20. Nguyen Hong Thao, "Maritime Delimitation and Fishery Cooperation in the Tonkin Gulf," *Ocean Development & International Law* 36 (2005): 29, http://community.middlebury.edu/~scs/docs/Nguyen%20Hong%20Thao-Maritime%20Delineation%20and%20Fishery%20Cooperation.pdf.

21. ITLOS, Case 16, 90–91.

22. *Arbitration between Guyana and Suriname, Award of 17 September 2007*, International Legal Materials, Vol. 47 (2008): 116, cited in ITLOS, Case 16, 74.

Figure 7. The Philippines' legal claim

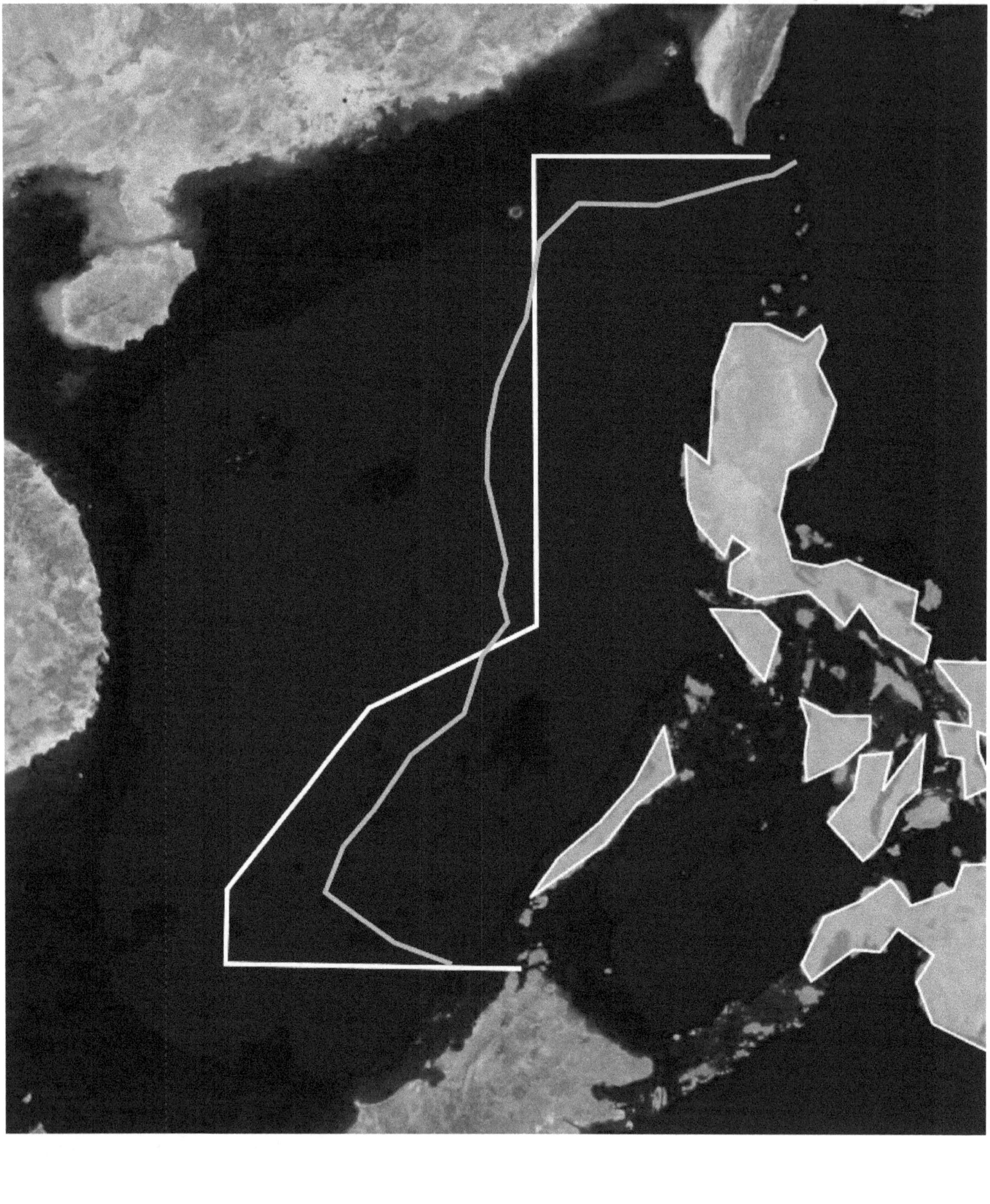

a line of equidistance until and unless that line is adjusted via arbitration or negotiation.[23]

The difference between the Philippines' actual legal claims in the South China Sea (green) and the claims most often depicted for it (white) are shown in Figure 7.

Vietnam

Vietnam's claims in the South China Sea have been the most overstated of those among the Southeast Asian claimants. Hanoi has taken considerable steps in recent years to clarify its claims in line with UNCLOS, but those developments have been largely overlooked.

The first major step toward clarifying Vietnam's claim occurred in 2003, when it signed a treaty with Indonesia delimiting the continental shelf and EEZ boundaries between southern Vietnam and the Tudjuh Archipelago.[24] That was followed the next year by the agreement with China delimiting their boundaries in the Gulf of Tonkin.

The next step in clarification was the dual submissions for Vietnam's continental shelf made to the CLCS in 2009. The joint submission with Malaysia for much of Vietnam's southern continental shelf received the lion's share of attention because it provoked China into presenting the nine-dash line map as an official protest. But equally important for the clarification of claims was the separate submission that Vietnam made for a section of its extended continental shelf farther to the north.[25]

The submission of these two claims to the CLCS implicitly proved that Hanoi no longer makes the vast claim shown on the textbook map, if it ever did, because they both fall short of that claim. This was confirmed by Vietnam's 2012 Law of the Sea, which, like the Philippines' 2009 baseline law, expressly declares that Vietnam claims only an EEZ of 200 nautical miles and a continental shelf of up to 350 nautical miles from its baselines.[26]

Aside from the maritime boundaries agreed to by treaty and the submissions made to the CLCS, there are two instances in which Vietnam's legal maritime claims do not match

---

23. One objection to this method could be that, for any number of reasons, even an adjusted equidistance line is inappropriate and should instead be replaced with the angle-bisector method of delimitation. This is applicable only to adjacent, not opposite, coasts. The former arguably exists between the Philippines and Malaysia. No South China Sea claimant has argued for this method, and in absence of proof to the contrary, the equidistance line must remain the default method of delimitation.

24. Agreement between the Government of the Socialist Republic of Vietnam and the Government of the Republic of Indonesia Concerning the Delimitation of the Continental Shelf Boundary, June 26, 2003, in United Nations Division for Ocean Affairs and the Law of the Sea, Office of Legal Affairs, *Law of the Sea Bulletin* 67 (2008): 39, http://www.un.org/Depts/los/doalos_publications/LOSBulletins/bulletinpdf/bulletin67e.pdf.

25. Socialist Republic of Vietnam, Submission to the Commission on the Limits of the Continental Shelf Pursuant to Article 76, Paragraph 8 of the United Nations Convention on the Law of the Sea 1982: Partial Submission in Respect of Vietnam's Extended Continental Shelf: North Area (VNM-N) (April 2009), http://www.un.org/Depts/los/clcs_new/submissions_files/vnm37_09/vnm2009n_executivesummary.pdf.

26. Vietnam, The Law of the Sea, Articles 15 and 17.

the 200-nautical-mile EEZ enumerated in its Law of the Sea. The first is the area between the mouth of the Gulf of Tonkin, where the agreement with China ends, and the northern end of Hanoi's individual extended continental shelf claim. Hanoi's EEZ and continental shelf overlap with that of China's Hainan Island in much of this area. Under the same principles earlier applied to the Philippines' claim, a legal claim by Hanoi here must be determined to be an equidistant line with Hainan. Once beyond China's potential 200-nautical-mile EEZ, a straight line connecting the limit of Vietnam's 200-nautical-mile EEZ to the northern end of its shelf submission is the only option in the absence of a further submission to the CLCS.

The second instance where Vietnam's remaining claim is not identical to its 200-nautical-mile EEZ is the space between the northern and southern continental shelf claims. Again, in the absence of a further submission, Vietnam's claim must be assumed to be as limited as possible. Therefore, it is limited to 200 nautical miles wherever possible. The limits of that EEZ must then be connected to the two continental shelves by the shortest possible distance.

The difference between Vietnam's actual legal claims in the South China Sea (blue) and the claims most often depicted for it (white) are shown in Figure 8.

China

After having clarified the claims of its neighbors, doing the same for China's legal maritime claim in the South China Sea is relatively simple. To the northwest, it consists of the line of demarcation in the Gulf of Tonkin agreed to with Vietnam. It then incorporates the same equidistant line between Hainan Island and the Vietnamese coastline that was used in determining Hanoi's claim. To the northwest, China's legal claim must be shown as the equidistant line between Taiwan and the Chinese coast on the one hand and the Philippines on the other.

In the center portion of China's claim in the South China Sea, its 200-nautical-mile EEZ does not overlap with that of any other country and therefore marks the farthest limit of its current legal claim, to both an EEZ and continental shelf, from its coastline. Beijing has submitted a claim to an extended continental shelf in the East China Sea beyond 200 nautical miles,[27] but has not done so in the South China Sea.

Continental Shelves versus EEZs

In attempting to clarify the legal claims of each party to the South China Sea disputes, continental shelves present a unique difficulty. UNCLOS establishes that each state's

27. People's Republic of China, Submission of the People's Republic of China Concerning the Outer Limits of the Continental Shelf beyond 200 Nautical Miles in Part of the East China Sea (December 14, 2012), http://www.un.org/Depts/los/clcs_new/submissions_files/chn63_12/executive%20summary_EN.pdf.

Figure 8. Vietnam's legal claim

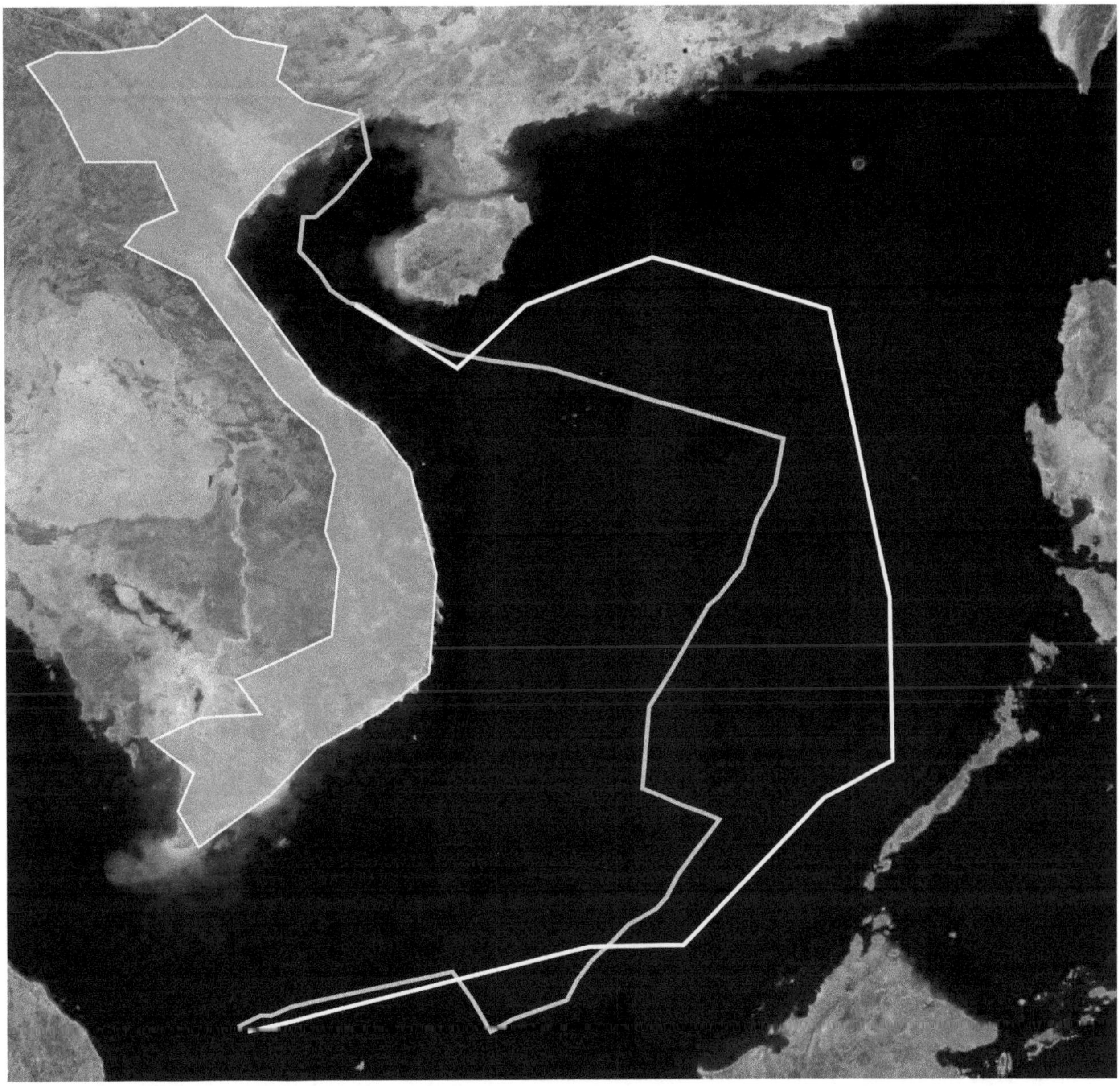

continental shelf automatically extends at least 200 nautical miles, to the same boundary as its EEZ, unless it overlaps with that of another state. In such cases, the general practice has been to demarcate both the EEZ and continental shelf at the same point, as Bangladesh and Myanmar requested in their case before ITLOS. This is not set in stone, but it is the most reasonable assumption in the absence of an explicit agreement between parties to the contrary. Therefore, in cases where EEZs and continental shelves overlap, this report treats the demarcation of a maritime boundary as the settlement of both an EEZ and continental shelf.

The other difficulty presented by continental shelves is that they can extend farther than an EEZ, up to 350 nautical miles as described above. UNCLOS sets out general rules for

Figure 9. China's legal claim

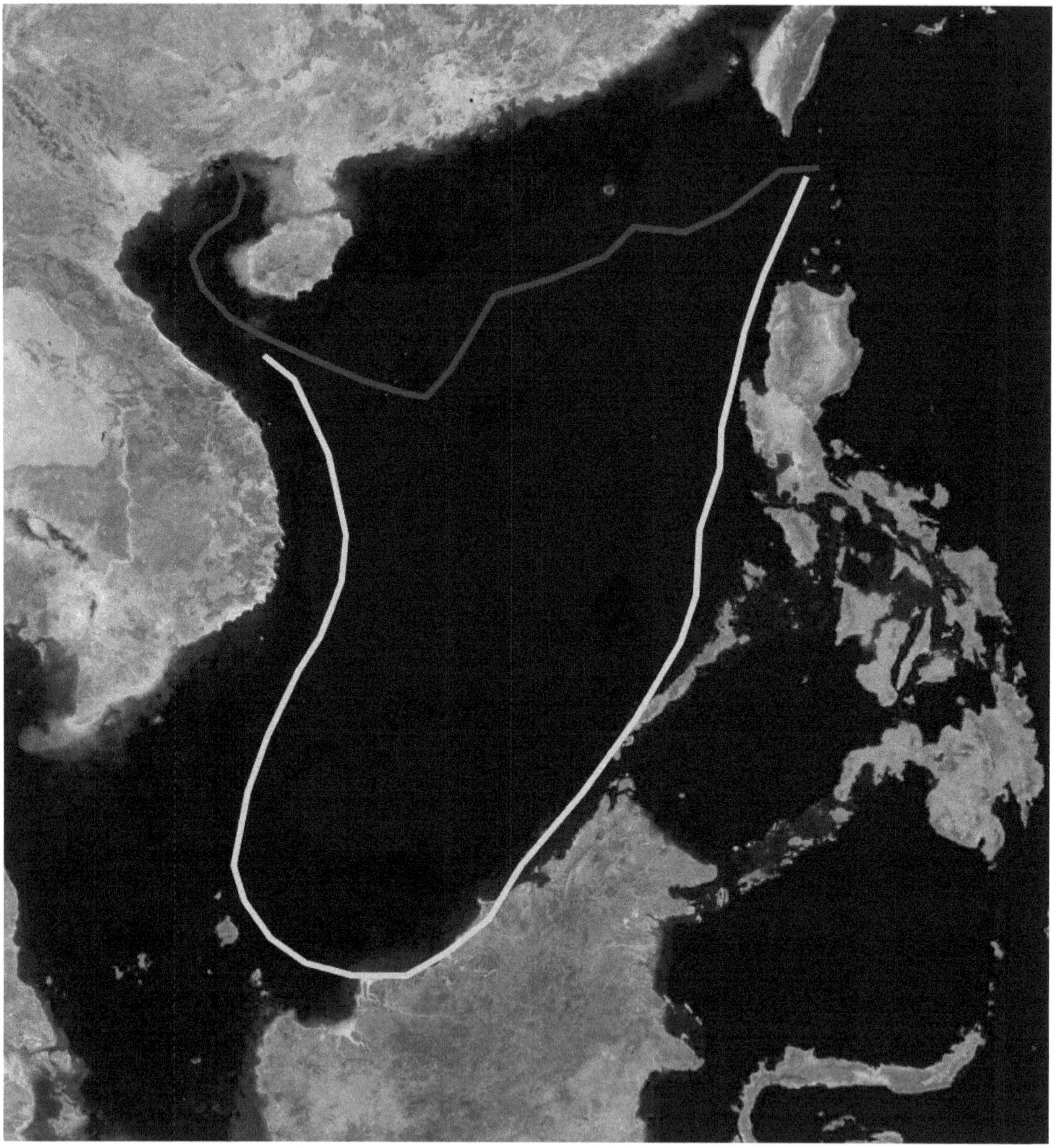

determining where a continental shelf may be delimited, if it extends beyond 200 nautical miles. However, that delimitation must be based on sophisticated studies of the seabed undertaken by the claimant state, the findings of which may be submitted to the CLCS as a claim.

States that are unable, for any reason, to undertake the necessary survey to submit a full claim to the CLCS may either provide a partial submission or postpone their submission until they are able to do so. This report therefore takes into account any extended continental shelf claims put forth in any detail by claimants, whether to the CLCS, as in the case of Vietnam and Malaysia, or not, as in the case of Brunei and the rest of Malaysia's shelf. However, in the absence of any submission, as in the case of China, the Philippines, or the remainder of Vietnam's continental shelf, the limits of the EEZ must also be assumed to be the limits of the continental shelf. This determination is made on the basis of the recognition that future submissions to the CLCS could expand some countries' claims and expand the area of dispute.

With the current legally permissible claims of each of the parties to the South China Sea disputes determined, it is now possible to get at the real heart of the dispute—the presence of hundreds of contested islets, rocks, and other features in the sea. The legal effects of these features on the disputes will be clarified in the following chapter, and a final determination of the maximum area of legal dispute determined.

3 Clarifying the Dispute

With the legal claims from the coastlines of each of the parties to the South China Sea disputes clarified, it is helpful to see how the situation would look were this the totality of the dispute. As Figure 10 shows, only a small fraction of the sea, where the claims of the Philippines, Malaysia, Brunei, and Vietnam overlap, is legally in dispute based on the EEZs and continental shelves off the claimants' coasts.

Unfortunately, the maritime disputes in the South China Sea are complicated, and changed, by simultaneous disputes over the land features of the Paracel Islands, Spratly Islands, Macclesfield Bank, and Scarborough Shoal, which sit in the middle of the sea.[1] This report does not, and indeed cannot, speak to the legality of claims to islands. UNCLOS and maritime law in general have nothing to say about overlapping disputes to land features, which can be decided only by the respective parties negotiating or by agreeing to submit to arbitration, likely by the International Court of Justice.

Although UNCLOS is silent on sovereignty over legally defined features, it is not silent on what determines whether a feature is an island. This determination is crucial to maritime delimitation because an island generates its own EEZ and continental shelf, just like a coastline, whereas features that are defined as rocks generate only a 12-nautical-mile territorial sea.[2]

Defining Islands

There are two requirements for a feature to be considered an island under UNCLOS. First, it must be above water at all times. Second, it must be capable of sustaining human habitation and/or an economic life of its own. If it meets the first requirement but not the second, it is legally a rock, not an island. If it does not even meet the first (that is, it is completely submerged at high tide), then it is neither a rock nor an island, does not generate any maritime claim of its own, and is not subject to an independent claim of sovereignty.[3] Such submerged features are legally under the control of that country on whose

1. This report will not include analysis of the Pratas Islands, which lie in the northern reaches of the South China Sea and are disputed by China and Taiwan. This is because no one claims them except Taiwan and China, and their only impact in delimitation is in the effect they have on the Philippines' EEZ, which has already been accounted for in Chapter 2.
2. UNCLOS, Article 121, http://www.un.org/Depts/los/convention_agreements/texts/unclos/part8.htm.
3. Ibid.

Figure 10. Legal claims from coastlines

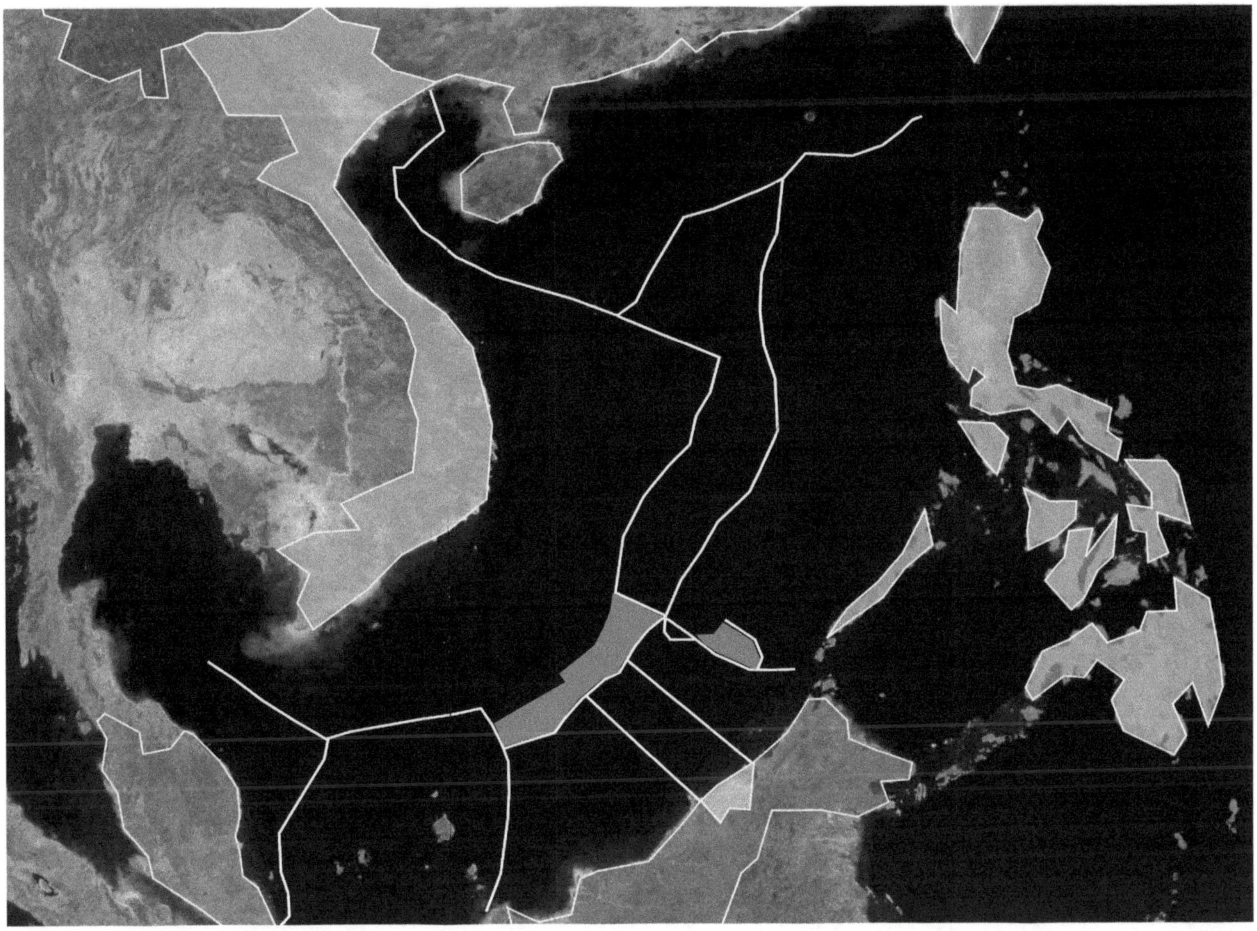

continental shelf they sit or are part of the international seabed if they lie outside any continental shelf claim.

The first step to defining the effects of the land features in the South China Sea on the area of dispute is necessarily to determine their status. The requirement for being an island or a rock is crystal clear: either the feature is submerged at high tide or it is not. The second is ambiguous. What is the minimum requirement for habitability? What about economic life? UNCLOS does not define these terms, and neither has any international court.

It may be a matter of common sense to say that a tiny rock (or four to six tiny rocks in the case of Scarborough Shoal) clearly cannot sustain human habitation. But this report's primary goal is to determine the maximum area of *legal* dispute in the South China Sea, not the area that common sense would dictate is in dispute. In other words, it may seem laughable to plant a flag on a sand dune and claim it is an island, but until the courts say otherwise, it is legal for countries to make that claim. This report therefore defines all features dry at high tide, no matter how small, as islands. A full list of specific features and their classification can be found in the Appendix.

Figure 11. Features[4]

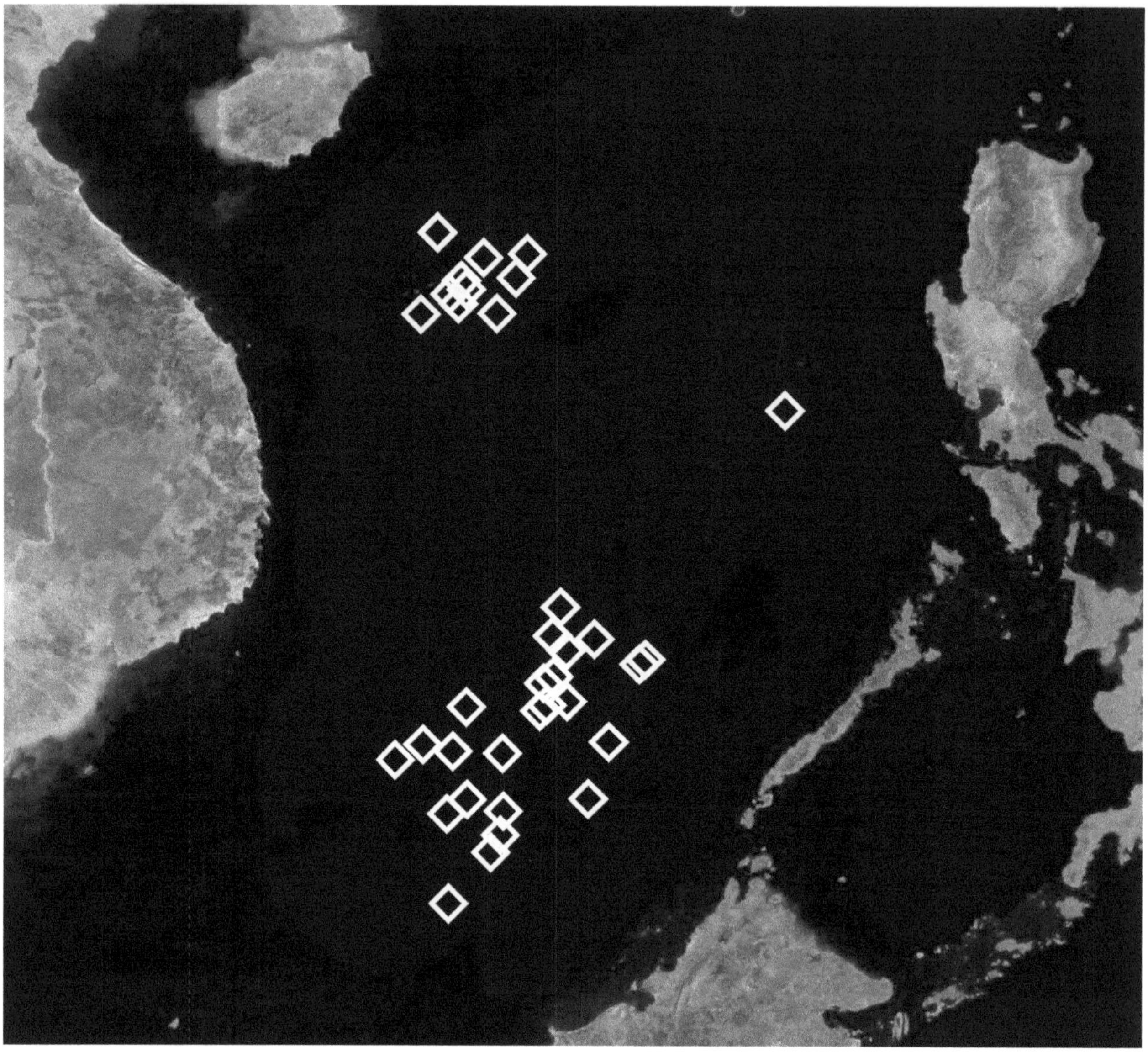

By that definition, there are 50 features in the South China Sea that available evidence suggests are likely above water at high tide,[5] and must therefore be assumed to generate an EEZ and continental shelf.

4. This map uses only one icon to represent the islands of the Crescent Group and another for the Amphitrite Group in the Paracels. The former is roughly 17 nautical miles at its widest and the latter approximately 12 nautical miles. Each contains at least six features that could be classified as islands with overlapping territorial seas. Each group's effect on delimitation is therefore essentially that of a single feature.

5. This determination is based on Monique Chemillier-Gendreau, *Sovereignty over the Paracel and Spratly Islands* (The Hague: Kluwer Law International, 2000), 17–18; David Hancox and Victor Prescott, *A Geographical Description of the Spratly Islands and an Account of Hydrographic Surveys amongst Those Islands*, Maritime Briefing, Vol. 1, No. 6 (Durham, UK: International Boundaries Research Unit, 1995), 3–30; Cire Sarr, "Digital Gazetteer of the Spratly Islands," August 2011, http://community.middlebury.edu/~scs/macand/gazetteer.htm; and publicly available satellite imagery from DigitalGlobe and NASA.

The Area of Legal Dispute

The final step in determining the maximum area of legal dispute in the South China Sea is to delimit the largest possible maritime claim generated by each of the 50 "islands." In most cases, this is a matter of determining the median point between a given island and the baselines of the nearest opposing coast. This is done under the same rationale as explained above in the determination of coastal claims.

In only one area where claims overlap is this formula not followed: the southwestern edge of the claim generated by the Spratly Islands, which extends beyond its median point with that generated from the Natuna Islands. This is because Indonesia's treaties with Malaysia and Vietnam already declare the extent of the Natunas' claim, which falls short of the would-be median line. The Spratlys' possible EEZ therefore extends all the way to that treaty boundary.

Only in the center of the sea, between the Paracel Islands and Scarborough Shoal, do the potential EEZs of some islands not overlap with those of opposing coasts. In these cases, the islands are given their full 200-nautical-mile claims.

It must also be noted that measurements for equidistant points are made from the best identifiable low-water mark of each individual feature. This means that the straight baselines that China declared for the Paracels in 1996 are not used. UNCLOS allows a country to declare archipelagic baselines, meaning straight baselines that extend between the islands of an archipelago, if the country is in fact an archipelagic state, like the Philippines. It does not, however, allow for the declaration of such baselines for a mainland country that claims sovereignty over a distant archipelago.[6]

The resulting map, shown in Figure 12, reveals the true area of dispute in the South China Sea under international law, broken out by whether the dispute emanates from the Paracels (red), Spratlys (green), or Scarborough Shoal (yellow).

Conclusion

Figure 12 shows that the area of legitimate dispute in the South China Sea encompasses approximately 298,000 square nautical miles (394,000 square miles). This is a substantial claim and it encompasses most, but not all, of the area within China's nine-dash line map, as shown in Figure 13.

It is important to reiterate that this is only the area of maximum dispute. This report makes no claim to be showing what a final delimitation in the South China Sea would look like. In fact, it would almost certainly show far less disputed area than Figure 12. Scarborough Shoal and the vast majority, if not all, of the Paracels and Spratlys could not be defined as habitable by most sober observers. After all, few of the features

6. UNCLOS, Article 47.

Figure 12. Maximum legal dispute

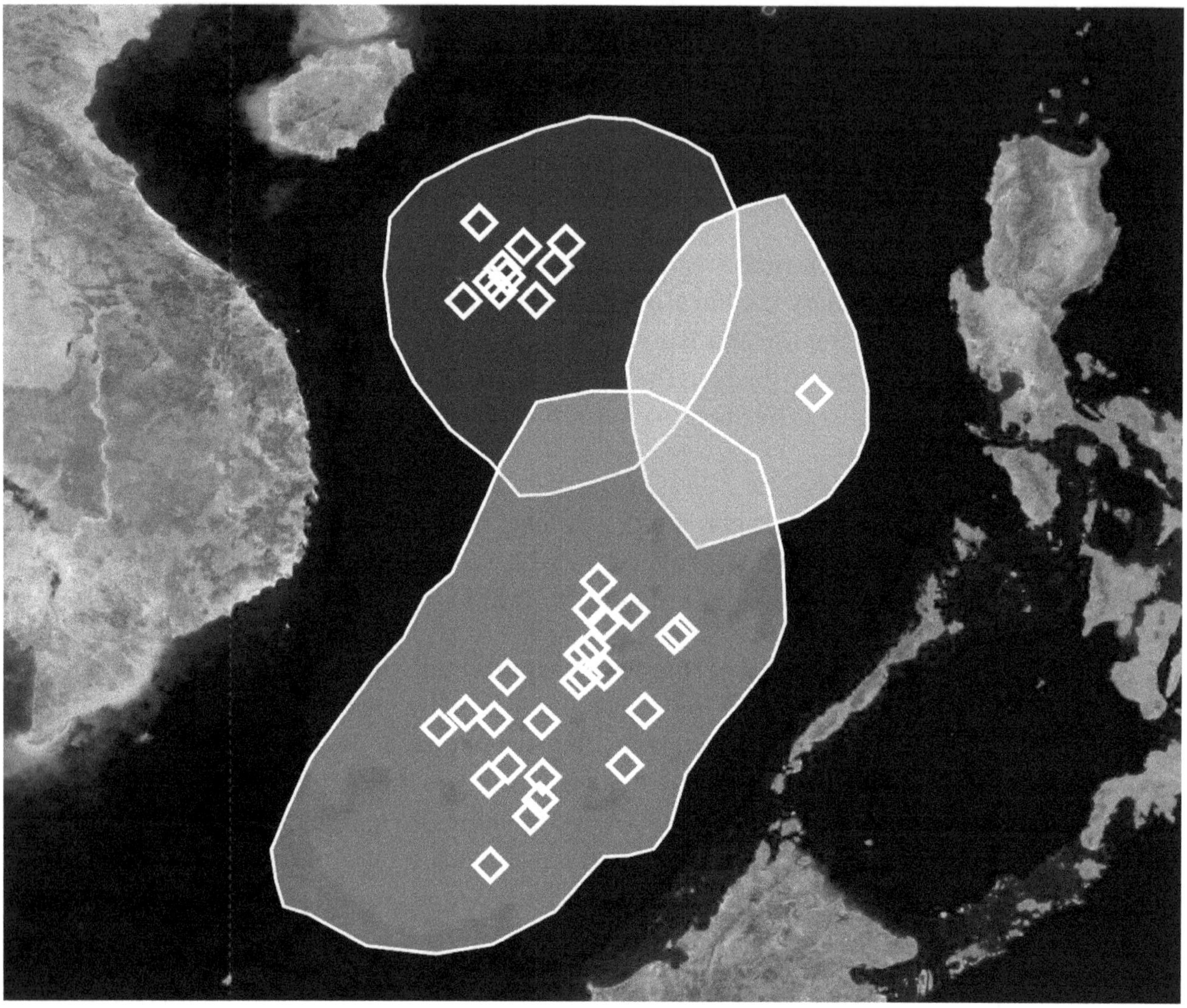

have vegetation, and only one of the Spratlys holds fresh water. But as explained earlier, the goal here is to define not the common-sense area of dispute but the maximum legal one.

Further, it is almost inconceivable that any international body would consider it equitable to give a speck of rock equal weight in delimitation with a country's shoreline. But as explained above, that is an argument that can be resolved only between claimants or in international tribunals. In the absence of such a resolution, everything within an equidistant line between the features and coastlines remains legally disputed.

The area of maximum dispute provides a jumping-off point for joint development and for negotiations between claimants. Anything outside this area undeniably falls within the jurisdiction of one, and only one, of the claimants. Any offers of joint development outside

Figure 13. Legal dispute vs. the nine-dash line

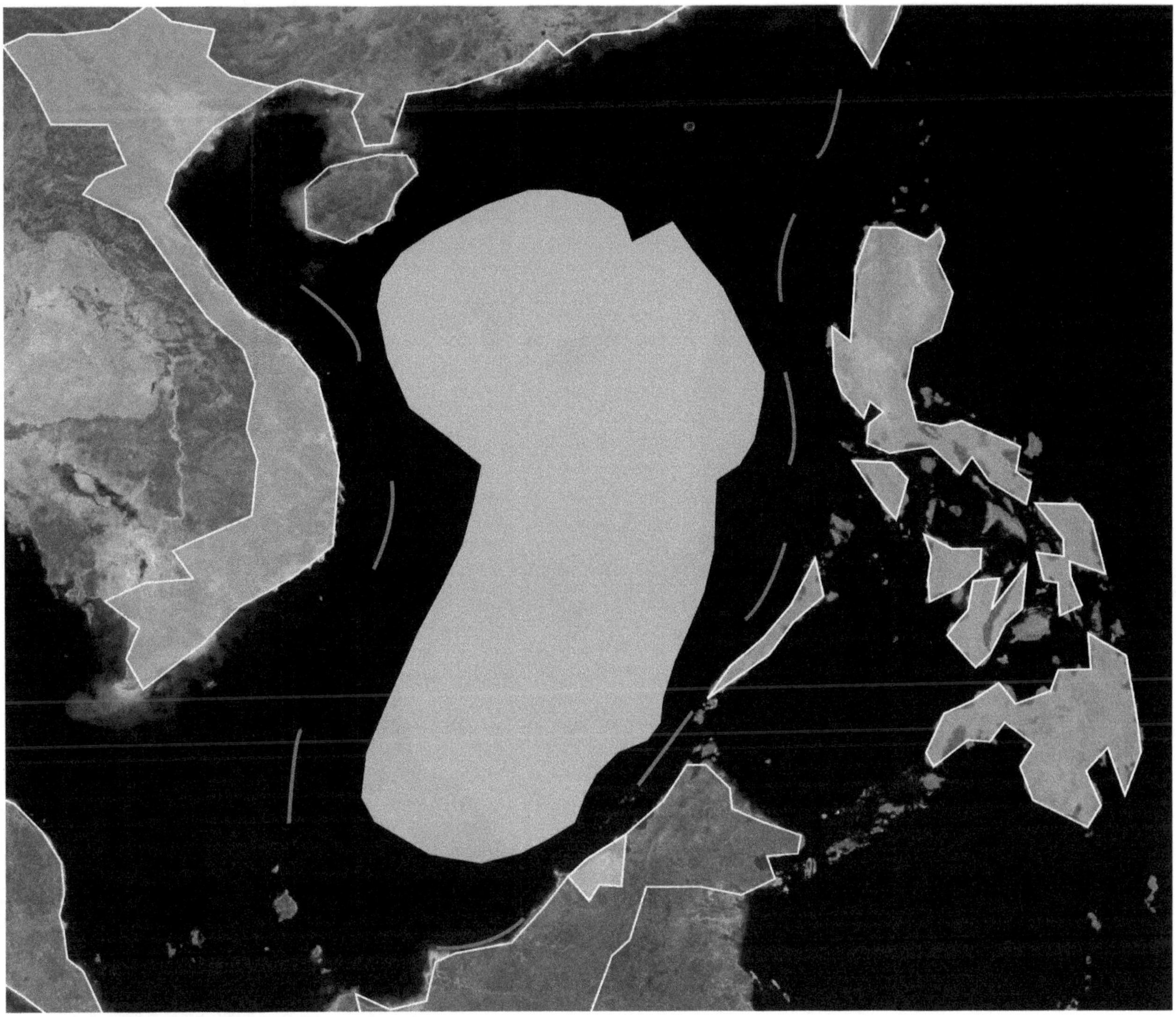

it are therefore without merit. This is the case that has been made by Vietnam and the Philippines repeatedly in recent years when China has offered areas just off their coasts for joint development. The geospatial analysis provided here should lend their arguments weight, both among neighbors and with the international community at large.

On June 25, 2012, the state-owned China National Offshore Oil Corporation (CNOOC) responded to ongoing tensions with Vietnam by declaring nine new offshore oil and gas blocks open for bids from foreign companies. The blocks were off the coast of Vietnam and the closest was located 230 nautical miles from China. All nine also overlapped with blocks previously created by Vietnam and leased to foreign companies, including ExxonMobil.

By simply overlaying these blocks with the map of the maximum legal dispute, it is obvious that CNOOC had no basis to claim most of the area that it put out for bid.

Figure 14. China National Offshore Oil Corporation blocks

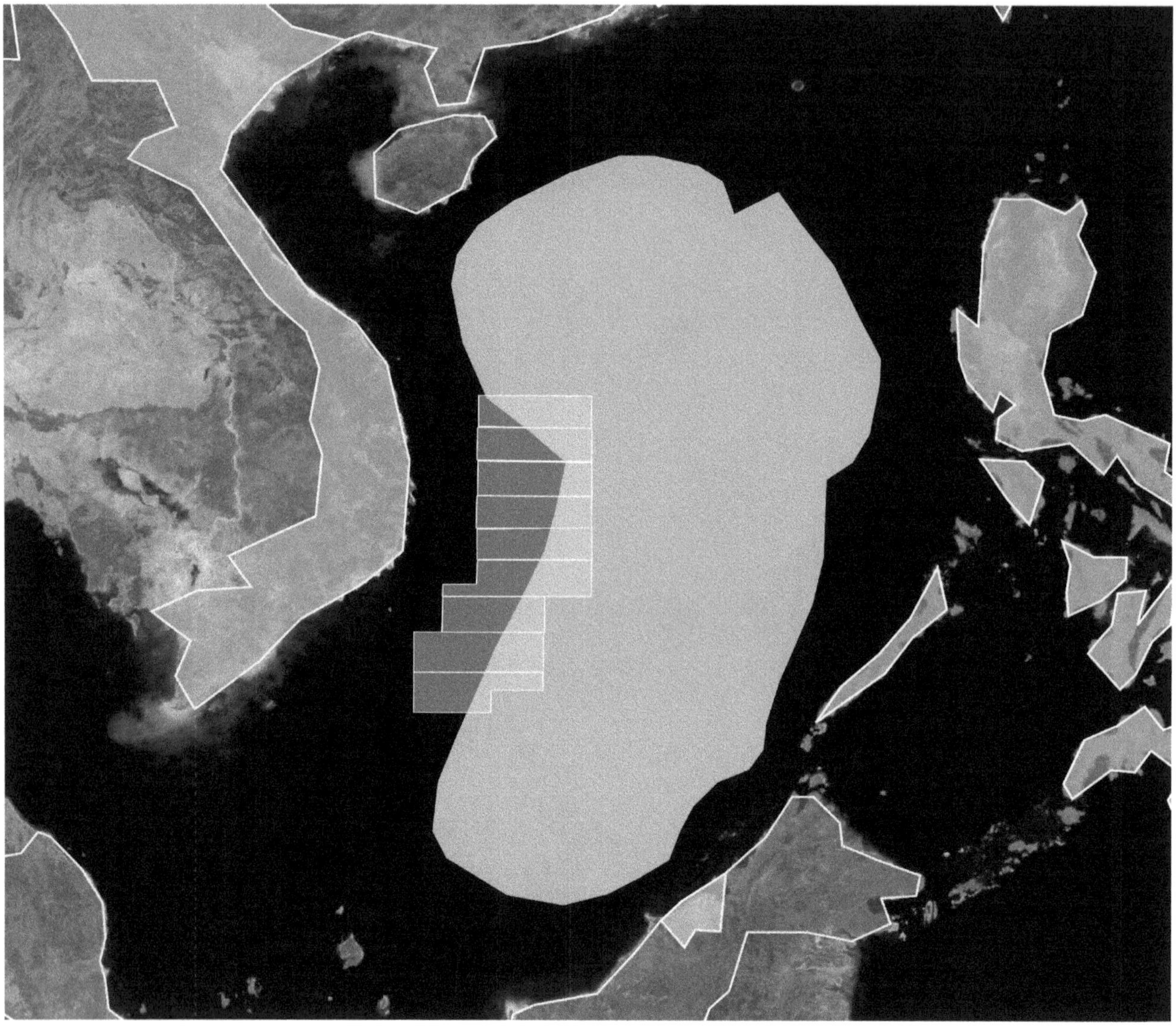

A few months earlier, on February 29, 2012, the Philippines invited foreign companies to take part in its long awaited fourth energy contracting round. This round opened bidding on 15 oil and gas blocks, two of which, Areas 3 and 4, drew protests from Beijing. Even though the blocks were just off the Philippine coast and hundreds of miles from China, Beijing claimed that they were within its legal maritime jurisdiction.

However, Figure 14 shows that the vast majority of oil and gas blocks created by Vietnam and the Philippines, including Areas 3 and 4, lie entirely in undisputed waters.

Rights to oil and gas is only one aspect of the South China Sea dispute that is clarified by determining the maximum area of legal dispute, but it is one of particular importance. It is also accurately treated as the keystone of potential joint development in the area. If

Figure 15. Philippine and Vietnam oil and gas blocks

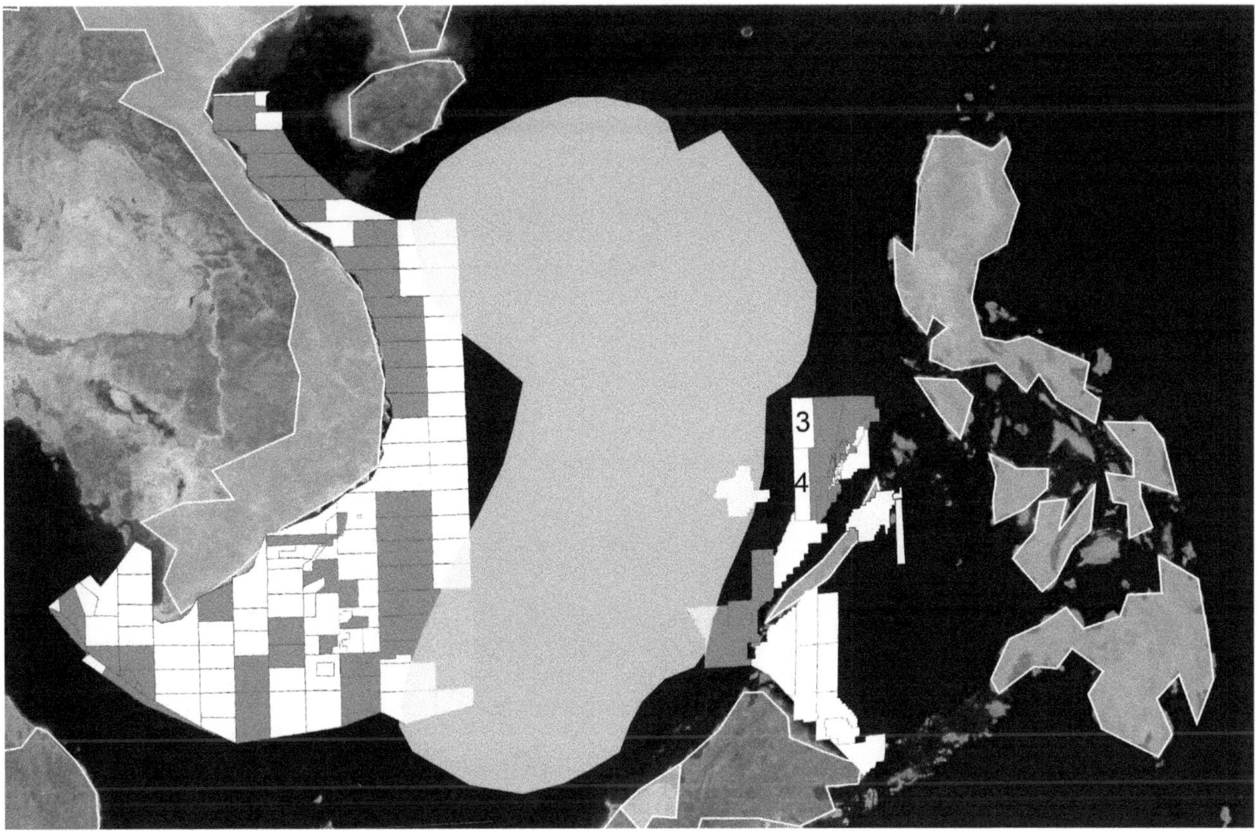

joint development is not restricted to the disputed area, along the lines shown above, it will never get off the ground.

All claimants should take the initiative to avoid provocative actions within this area of maximum dispute. Any new oil and gas development, any new settlement or building on disputed features, and any needlessly aggressive military exercises should be excluded from these disputed areas. This may be a tough pill to swallow, but it comes with the benefit of a moral and legal high ground and an ironclad defense for those activities a country performs in its jurisdiction outside of the disputed waters.

Appendix: Classification of Islands and Rocks

The following is a list of features in the South China Sea and their classification as islands or rocks according to the criteria set forth in the "Defining Islands" section of Chapter 3. This list does not include every feature in the South China Sea, but it does include, to the best of the author's knowledge, every feature at least partially above water at low tide and those submerged features that have been named and/or charted in publicly available sources. This list uses the English names for features, except where they do not exist or names in other languages have become the norm in international use.

The Pratas Islands do not fall within the scope of this report. But there are two other features outside of the Paracel and Spratly chains that do: Macclesfield Bank and Scarborough Shoal. The former is entirely submerged and therefore capable of generating neither a territorial sea nor an EEZ. The latter, with four to six rocks above water at high tide, meets this report's minimum definition of an island. The tables that follow provide classifications for the Paracels and Spratlys.

The Paracels

Feature name	*Classified as an island?*
Amphitrite Group	Yes
Bombay Reef	Yes
Bremen Bank	No
Crescent Group	Yes
Discovery Reef	Yes
Iltis Bank	No
Lincoln Island	Yes
North Reef	Yes
Passu Keah	Yes
Triton Island	Yes
Vuladdore Reef	Yes

The Spratlys

Feature name	*Classified as an island?*	*Feature name*	*Classified as an island?*
Alicia Annie Reef	Yes	Loaita Cay	No
Alison Reef	No	Loaita Island	Yes
Amboyna Cay	Yes	Louisa Reef	No
Ardasier Reef	Yes	Loveless Reef	No
Baker Reef	No	Lys Shoal	No
Ban Than Reef	No	Mariveles Reef	Yes
Barque Canada Reef	Yes	Menzies Reef	No
Bombay Shoal	No	Mischief Reef	No
Boxall Reef	No	Namyit Island	Yes
Brown Reef	No	Nanshan Island	Yes
Central Reef	Yes	North Reef	No
Collins Reef	Yes	Northeast Cay	Yes
Commodore Reef	Yes	Northeast Investigator Shoal	No
Cornwallis South Reef	No	Owen Shoal	No
Cuarteron Reef	Yes	Pearson Reefs	Yes
Dallas Reef	No	Pennsylvania North Reef	No
Discovery Great Reef	No	Petley Reef	No
Discovery Small Reef	No	Pigeon Reef	No
East Reef	No	Prince Consort Bank	No
Eldad Reef	No	Prince of Wales Bank	No
Erica Reef	No	Reed Bank	No
Fiery Cross Reef	Yes	Rifleman Bank	No
First Thomas Shoal	Yes	Royal Captain Shoal	No
Flat Island	Yes	Royal Charlotte Reef	Yes
Gaven Reefs	Yes	Sabina Shoal	No
Grainger Bank	No	Sand Cay	Yes
Half Moon Shoal	No	Second Thomas Reef	No
Hardy Reef	No	Sin Cowe Island	Yes
Higgen Reef	No	South Reef	No
Holiday Reef	No	Southern Reefs	No
Hopps Reef	No	Southwest Cay	Yes
Hughes Reef	No	Spratly Island	Yes
Investigator Shoal	No	Subi Reef	No
Iroquois Reef	No	Swallow Reef	Yes
Irving Reef	No	Templer Bank	No
Itu Aba Island	Yes	Thitu Island	Yes
Jackson Reef	No	Trident Shoal	No
Johnson South Reef	Yes	Union Banks	No
Kennan Reef	No	Vanguard Bank	No
Ladd Reef	No	West Reef	No
Lankiam Cay	Yes	West York Island	Yes
Lansdowne Reef	No	Western Reef	No
Livock Reef	No	Whitson Reef	Yes

About the Author

Gregory B. Poling is a research associate with the Sumitro Chair for Southeast Asia Studies and the Pacific Partners Initiative at CSIS, where he manages projects that focus on U.S. foreign policy in the Asia Pacific, with a special focus on the member countries of the Association of Southeast Asian Nations. His current research interests include disputes in the South China Sea, democratization in Southeast Asia, and Asian multilateralism.

Mr. Poling is coauthor of *From Strength to Empowerment: The Next Generation of U.S.-Malaysia Relations* (CSIS, May 2012) and *Sustainable Energy Futures in Southeast Asia* (December 2012). Before joining CSIS, he lived and worked in China as an English-language teacher. He received an MA in international affairs from American University, a BA in history and philosophy from Saint Mary's College of Maryland, and studied at Fudan University in Shanghai.

www.ingramcontent.com/pod-product-compliance
Ingram Content Group UK Ltd.
Pitfield, Milton Keynes, MK11 3LW, UK
UKHW051418150926
475561UK00005B/233

9 781442 224858